PICTUREPEDIA

NOTE TO PARENTS

This book is part of PICTUREPEDIA, a completely
new kind of information series for children.
Its unique combination of pictures and words
encourages children to use their eyes to discover and
explore the world, while introducing them to a wealth
of basic knowledge. Clear, straightforward text
explains each picture thoroughly and provides
additional information about the topic.

'Looking it up' becomes an easy task with
PICTUREPEDIA, an ideal first reference for all types of
schoolwork. Because PICTUREPEDIA is also entertaining,
children will enjoy reading its words and looking
at its pictures over and over again. You can encourage
and stimulate further inquiry by helping your child
pose simple questions for the whole family to
'look up' and answer together.

SPACE

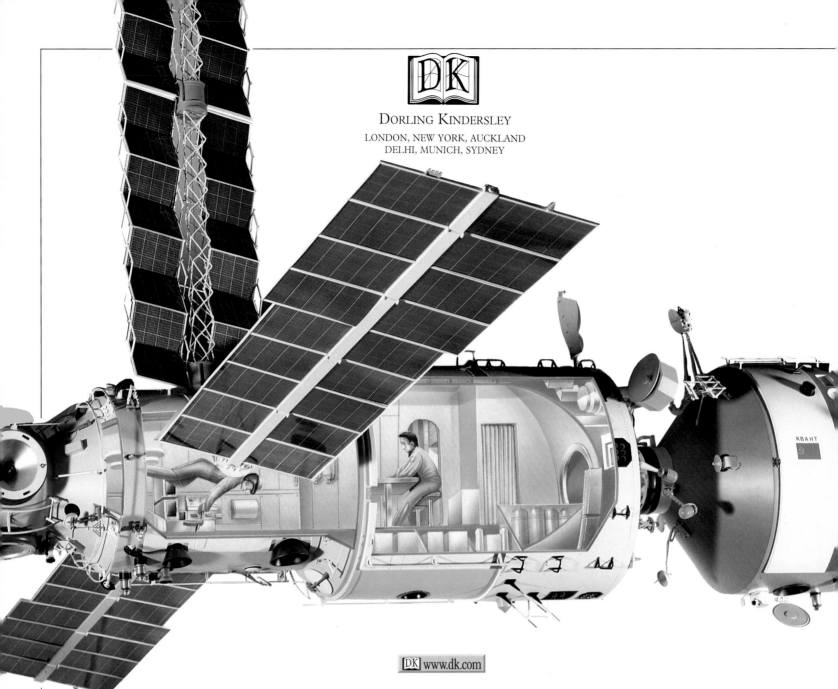

DK

DORLING KINDERSLEY

LONDON, NEW YORK, AUCKLAND
DELHI, MUNICH, SYDNEY

DK www.dk.com

First published in Great Britain in 1992
by Dorling Kindersley Limited, London

This updated edition published in 2000 by:

Dorling Kindersley Limited
9 Henrietta Street, London WC2E 8PS, Great Britain

Dorling Kindersley Publishing Pty Limited
(A.C.N. 078 414 445)
118-120 Pacific Highway, St Leonards NSW 2065, Australia

Dorling Kindersley (India) Pvt. Ltd.
102/3 Kaushalya Park, Hauz Khas, New Delhi 110016, India

Copyright © 1992/2000 Dorling Kindersley Limited, London

A CIP catalogue record for this
book is available from the British Library.

ISBN 0 7513 6900 4

Reproduction by Colourscan, Singapore
Printed and bound by L. Rex Printing Company Limited, China

SPACE

United States

DK

A DORLING KINDERSLEY BOOK

CONTENTS

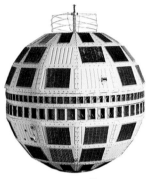

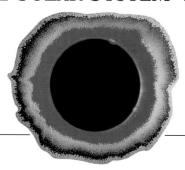

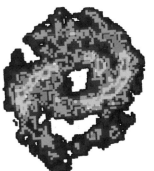

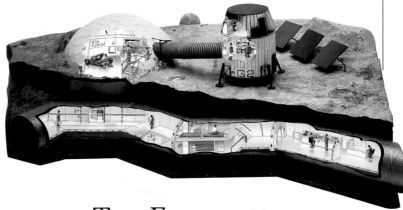

Into the Universe

People have always been curious about the things they could see up in the sky. On a clear night it is possible to see the Moon and hundreds, or even thousands, of stars. People who study the stars and planets are called astronomers. The universe is made up of galaxies, stars, planets, moons, and other bodies scattered throughout space.

Comet

Supernova

Arrows shot from a fire basket

Sky Watcher
This is Galileo Galilei. He lived in Italy about 350 years ago. He was one of the first people to use the telescope to study the Moon and planets. He proved that the Earth moves round the Sun.

Up into Space
The first rockets were invented in China over 800 years ago and worked by using gunpowder, like fireworks today. Years later, rockets were made that could travel fast enough to take people into space.

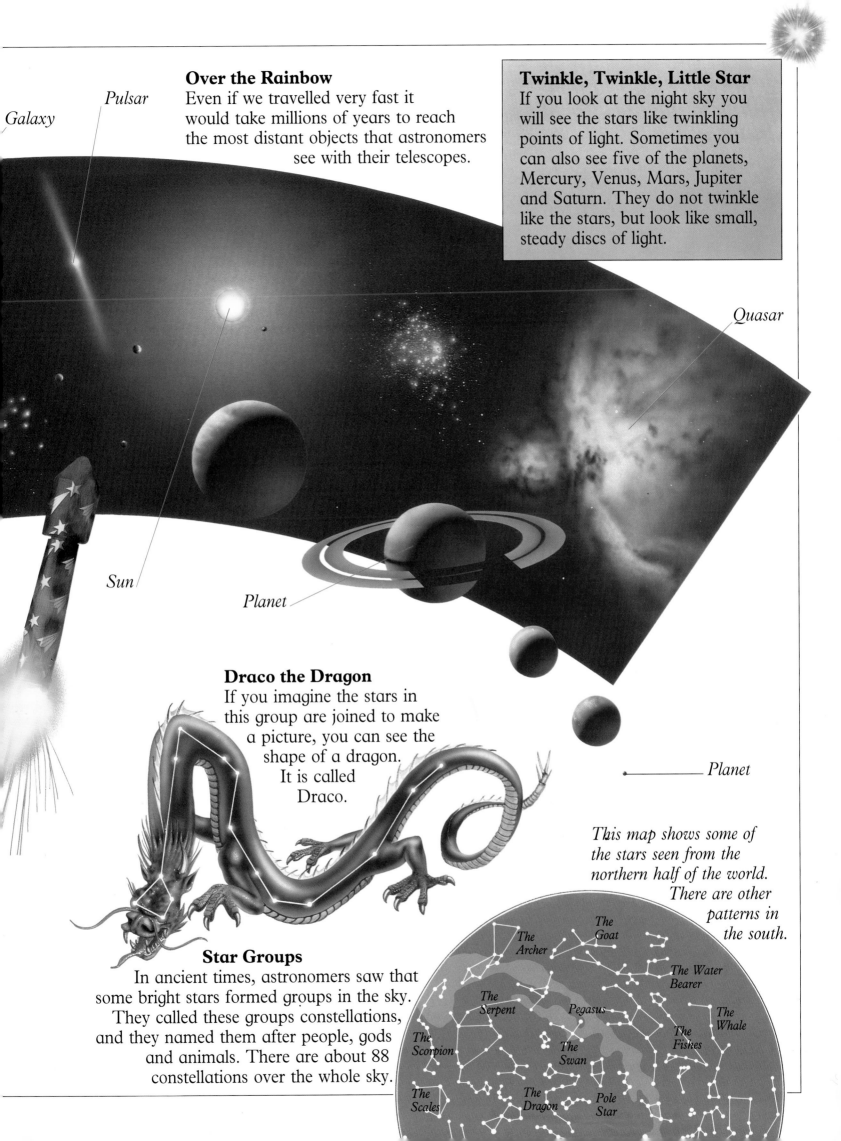

Galaxy

Pulsar

Over the Rainbow
Even if we travelled very fast it would take millions of years to reach the most distant objects that astronomers see with their telescopes.

Quasar

Sun

Planet

Draco the Dragon
If you imagine the stars in this group are joined to make a picture, you can see the shape of a dragon. It is called Draco.

Planet

This map shows some of the stars seen from the northern half of the world. There are other patterns in the south.

Star Groups
In ancient times, astronomers saw that some bright stars formed groups in the sky. They called these groups constellations, and they named them after people, gods and animals. There are about 88 constellations over the whole sky.

The Archer

The Goat

The Serpent

Pegasus

The Water Bearer

The Scorpion

The Swan

The Fishes

The Whale

The Scales

The Dragon

Pole Star

CONSTELLATIONS

The groups of stars we see in the sky are called constellations. These groups have Latin names, such as Ursa Major, which means Great Bear. When you first go outside to look for a constellation you may find it difficult to spot among all the stars in the sky. The Earth is spinning round very slowly so that over a few hours it may seem as if the stars have moved across the sky, but if you gaze for long enough you can pick out the patterns made by the brightest stars.

Leaping Lion
If you imagine the stars in a group have been joined to make a picture, you will see why this constellation is called Leo the Lion.

Northern Hemisphere

BOÖTES
The Herdsman

URSA MAJOR
The Great Bear

LYNX
The Lynx

LEO
The Lion

GEMINI
The Twins

Sky Lights
These two pictures show what the night sky would look like if you were standing, looking up, in the northern half of the world at one time of the year.

Light-Years
Huge distances are often measured by astronomers in light-years. A light-year is the distance a beam of light can travel in a year. Light takes eight minutes to reach the Earth from the Sun. Light from the next nearest star takes over four years!

CYGNUS
The Swan

LACERTA
The Lizard

ARIES
The Ram

PEGASUS
The Flying Horse

DELPHINUS
The Dolphin

PISCES
The Fish

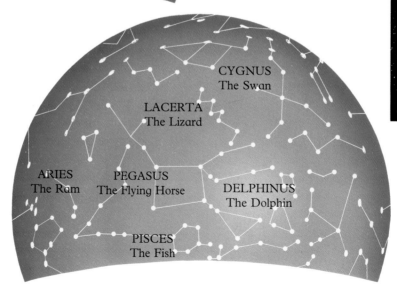

Orion the Hunter
The constellation of Orion can be seen from most parts of the world. The three stars close together form Orion's belt. Below the belt is his sword.

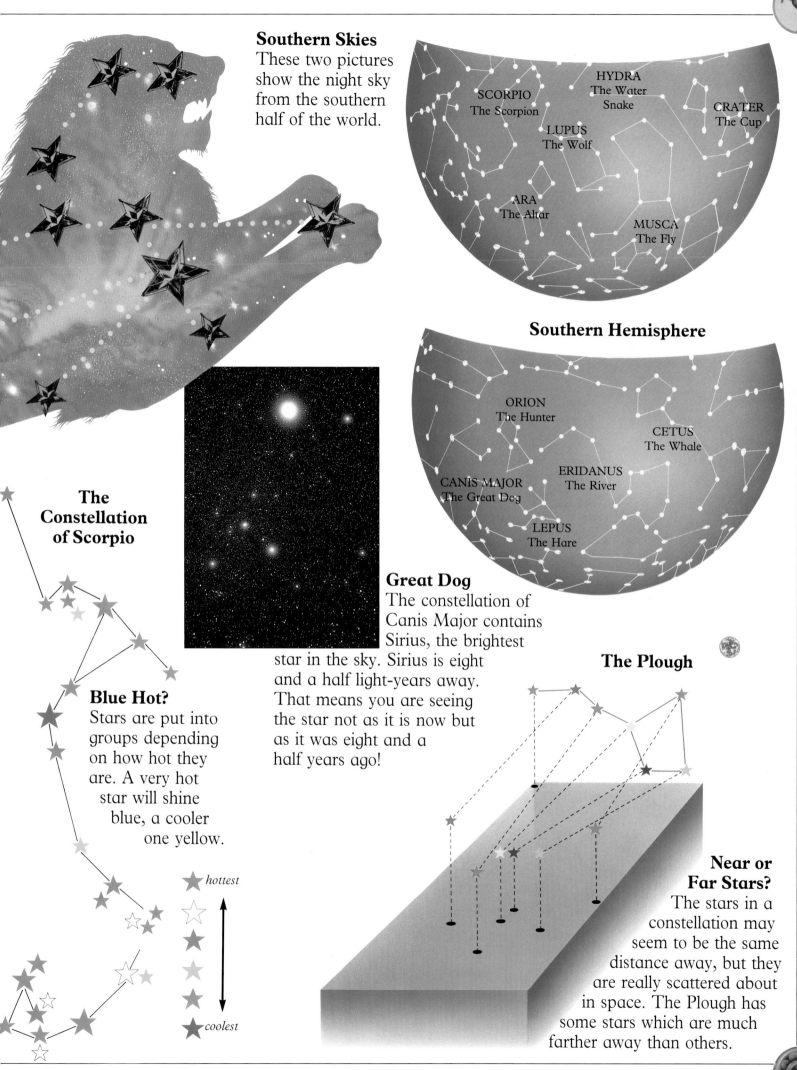

Southern Skies

These two pictures show the night sky from the southern half of the world.

SCORPIO
The Scorpion

HYDRA
The Water Snake

CRATER
The Cup

LUPUS
The Wolf

ARA
The Altar

MUSCA
The Fly

Southern Hemisphere

ORION
The Hunter

CETUS
The Whale

ERIDANUS
The River

CANIS MAJOR
The Great Dog

LEPUS
The Hare

The Constellation of Scorpio

Blue Hot?

Stars are put into groups depending on how hot they are. A very hot star will shine blue, a cooler one yellow.

hottest

coolest

Great Dog

The constellation of Canis Major contains Sirius, the brightest star in the sky. Sirius is eight and a half light-years away. That means you are seeing the star not as it is now but as it was eight and a half years ago!

The Plough

Near or Far Stars?

The stars in a constellation may seem to be the same distance away, but they are really scattered about in space. The Plough has some stars which are much farther away than others.

LIFT-OFF

Rockets were invented in China a long time ago. They looked a bit like arrows and worked by burning gunpowder which burns up very quickly, so the rockets did not travel very far. Since then, people have tried many ways of sending rockets up into space. In modern rockets, two liquid fuels are used. They mix together and burn. Then the hot gas shoots out of the tail, pushing the rocket up and away.

V-2 Rocket
1944

Gemini
Titan 1964

The Fly!
In 1931 Johannes Winkler launched his HW-1 rocket. It went two metres into the air, turned over and fell back to the ground. A month later he tried again and this time it climbed to 90 metres and landed 200 metres away.

3, 2, 1, Fire!
Two hundred years ago, soldiers used rockets like this. They were called Congreve rockets.

See It Go!
If you blow up a balloon and let it go without tying a knot in the neck, the air will rush out very quickly. When the air goes out one way it pushes the balloon the other way – just like a rocket!

Saturn Power
Saturn 5 is the biggest rocket ever built. It is as tall as a 30-storey building! It carried the first American astronauts to land on the Moon.

The stabilizing fins keep the rocket on course.

Five rocket engines

Fuel tank

Up, Up . . .
How far can you throw a ball? About 15 or 20 metres? It doesn't go on for ever because the Earth's gravity pulls it back down again.

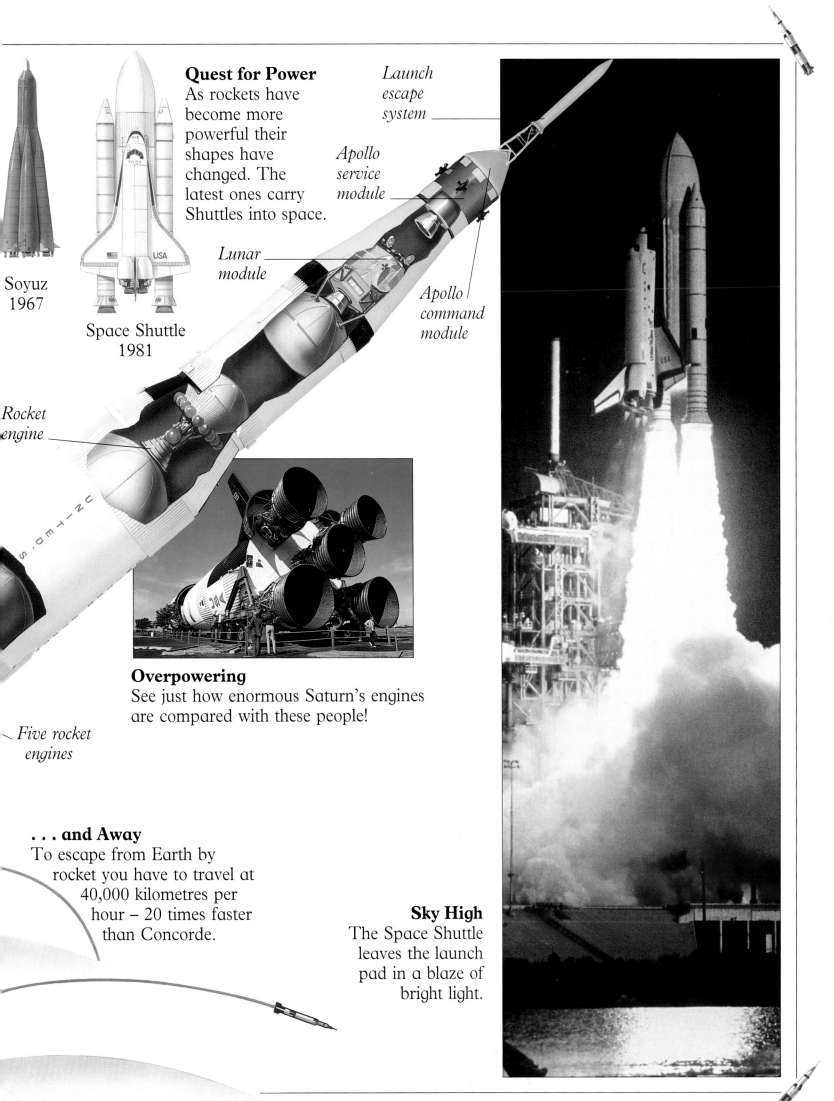

Quest for Power
As rockets have become more powerful their shapes have changed. The latest ones carry Shuttles into space.

Soyuz 1967

Space Shuttle 1981

Launch escape system

Apollo service module

Lunar module

Apollo command module

Rocket engine

Five rocket engines

Overpowering
See just how enormous Saturn's engines are compared with these people!

. . . and Away
To escape from Earth by rocket you have to travel at 40,000 kilometres per hour – 20 times faster than Concorde.

Sky High
The Space Shuttle leaves the launch pad in a blaze of bright light.

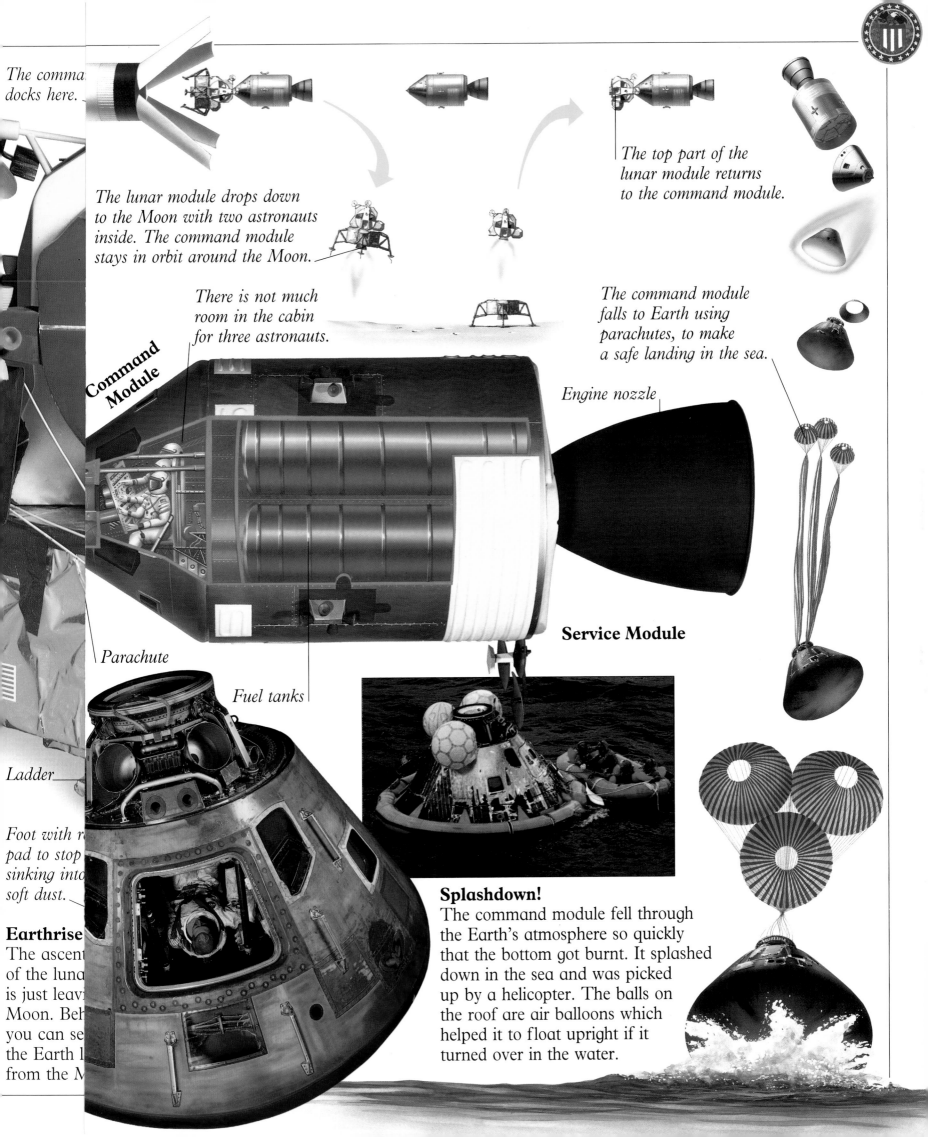

The comma...
docks here.

*The lunar module drops down
to the Moon with two astronauts
inside. The command module
stays in orbit around the Moon.*

*The top part of the
lunar module returns
to the command module.*

*There is not much
room in the cabin
for three astronauts.*

*The command module
falls to Earth using
parachutes, to make
a safe landing in the sea.*

**Command
Module**

Engine nozzle

Service Module

Parachute

Fuel tanks

Ladder

*Foot with r...
pad to stop
sinking into
soft dust.*

Earthrise
The ascen...
of the luna...
is just leavi...
Moon. Beh...
you can se...
the Earth l...
from the M...

Splashdown!
The command module fell through
the Earth's atmosphere so quickly
that the bottom got burnt. It splashed
down in the sea and was picked
up by a helicopter. The balls on
the roof are air balloons which
helped it to float upright if it
turned over in the water.

THE SOLAR SYSTEM

This shows the order of the planets and their distances from the Sun. It does not show their sizes.

The word 'solar' means belonging to the Sun. The Sun is the centre of a family of planets called the solar system. Nine planets and their moons move round the Sun in huge, oval-shaped orbits. At the same time they all spin round like tops. The four inner planets are like rocky balls, the outer ones are liquid or gas, except icy Pluto. The Earth is one of the inner planets. Without the heat and light from the Sun, there would be no life on Earth.

Prominence

Core

Radiative layer

Chromosphere

Photosphere

Corona

Sun Burn
If you could cut a slice of the Sun, you would see the core and the layers of burning gas around it.

Layers of Gas
This photograph shows the layers of gas around the Sun. Added colours make the layers easier to see. It was taken from Earth and shows a solar eclipse, which happens when the Moon seems to cover the Sun.

SATURN

Ulysses

Sun Snaps
The space probe Ulysses flew over the Sun and took pictures. A space probe has no people on it.

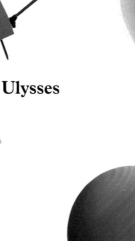

NEPTUNE

URANUS

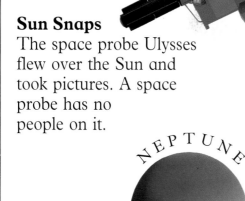

PLUTO

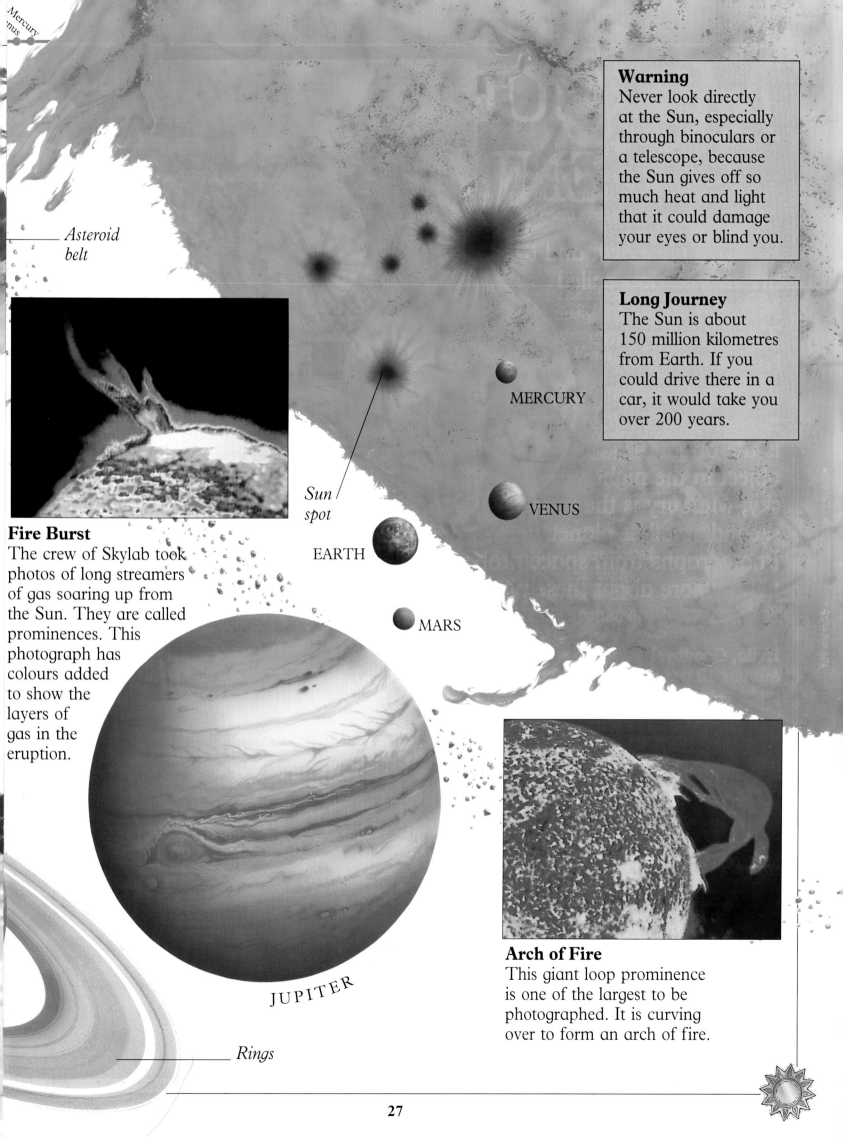

Asteroid belt

Long Journey
The Sun is about 150 million kilometres from Earth. If you could drive there in a car, it would take you over 200 years.

MERCURY

Sun spot

VENUS

Fire Burst
The crew of Skylab took photos of long streamers of gas soaring up from the Sun. They are called prominences. This photograph has colours added to show the layers of gas in the eruption.

EARTH

MARS

JUPITER

Rings

Arch of Fire
This giant loop prominence is one of the largest to be photographed. It is curving over to form an arch of fire.

THE RED PLANET

Viking Spacecraft

The Viking lander is folded into a capsule on the spacecraft.

The red planet is Mars. It is called the red planet because the soil and rocks are red. Light winds blow the dust around, which makes the sky look pink. People once thought there was life on Mars, but nothing living has been found so far.

Two Viking spacecraft, controlled from Earth, have visited Mars to find out what it is like. Perhaps one day people from Earth may go and live there because it is the planet most like our own.

It leaves the orbiter and begins its journey down to Mars.

The television camera takes a series of pictures as it moves round.

It moves so fast that it gets very hot.

A parachute is used to slow it down, and then the heat shield drops off.

This remote control arm is used to collect samples of Mars soil.

Tight Fit
The Viking lander fits into a capsule on the spacecraft. With its legs folded up, it looks a bit like a tortoise inside its shell.

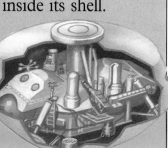

The legs unfold, and rockets are used as brakes for a soft landing.

The Viking Lander

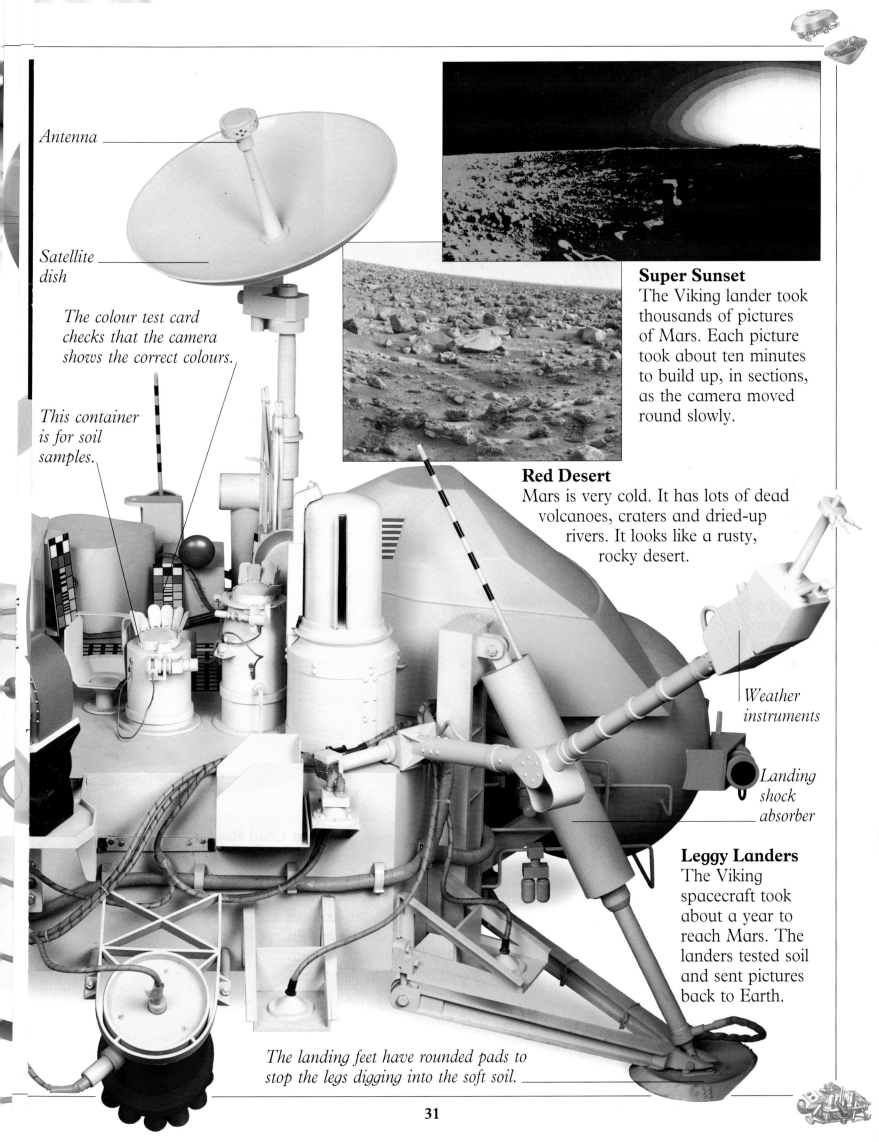

Antenna

Satellite dish

The colour test card checks that the camera shows the correct colours.

This container is for soil samples.

Super Sunset
The Viking lander took thousands of pictures of Mars. Each picture took about ten minutes to build up, in sections, as the camera moved round slowly.

Red Desert
Mars is very cold. It has lots of dead volcanoes, craters and dried-up rivers. It looks like a rusty, rocky desert.

Weather instruments

Landing shock absorber

Leggy Landers
The Viking spacecraft took about a year to reach Mars. The landers tested soil and sent pictures back to Earth.

The landing feet have rounded pads to stop the legs digging into the soft soil.

SKY WATCHING

If you look up at the sky on a clear night you can see hundreds of stars and, sometimes, the Moon. But if you use binoculars or a telescope you can see even more – for example, the planets and the craters on the Moon.

When astronomers study the universe they use huge radio telescopes, some with dishes, to help them to see far, far away, and to gather information from space. The Hubble Space Telescope is the largest telescope to be put into space. It can take clear pictures of stars and galaxies because it orbits 600 km above the Earth's murky atmosphere.

Clearly Venus
This photograph of Venus was taken by the Pioneer Venus Orbiter. It used radar to get a clear picture through the thick clouds around Venus. The signals were sent back to Earth to a radio telescope where this picture was produced.

Solar panel

Radio telescope

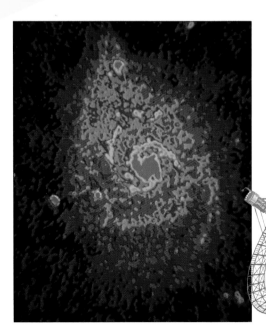

Whirligig
This radio map of the Whirlpool galaxy was taken by a radio telescope. The added colours show the spiral arms of the galaxy.

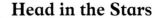

Head in the Stars
Through a telescope you can see the Horsehead nebula. This picture has false colours added but it looks nearly as bright without them.

Star Belt
This photograph, taken through a small telescope, shows part of the constellation of Orion – also called 'The Hunter'.

Flap door

Small mirror

Star Cluster
This photograph was taken by the Hubble Space Telescope and it shows a star cluster.

Main mirror

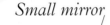

Star Light
This natural colour photograph was taken from an observatory. It shows the Orion nebula which is a cloud of dust and gas lit from inside by newly born stars.

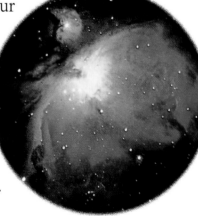

Double Hubble
The Hubble has two mirrors – the largest is 2.4 metres wide and 30 centimetres thick. At first the mirrors did not work quite as well as they should have done, but astronauts from the Shuttle later corrected them.

Antenna

Look Out
An observatory is a place where astronomers work. They are usually away from big cities where there are no street lights and the air is clear.

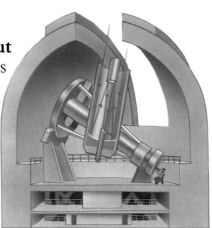

FLOATING WORLDS

One day in the future, astronauts from several countries will be living and working on the International Space Station (ISS). But ordinary people too may soon spend time in space – in a Japanese-built space hotel. There are also plans to build space colonies where people can live in space for a lifetime, just visiting the Earth for holidays!

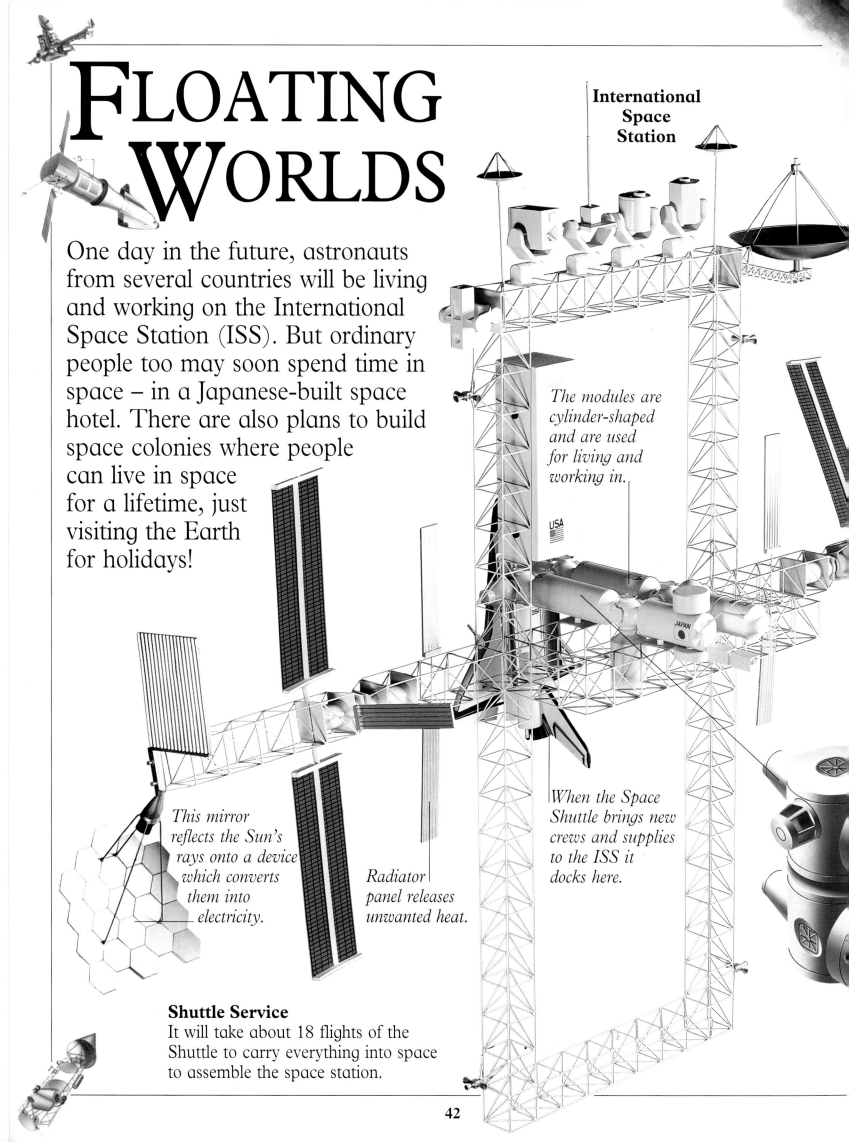

International Space Station

The modules are cylinder-shaped and are used for living and working in.

This mirror reflects the Sun's rays onto a device which converts them into electricity.

Radiator panel releases unwanted heat.

When the Space Shuttle brings new crews and supplies to the ISS it docks here.

Shuttle Service
It will take about 18 flights of the Shuttle to carry everything into space to assemble the space station.

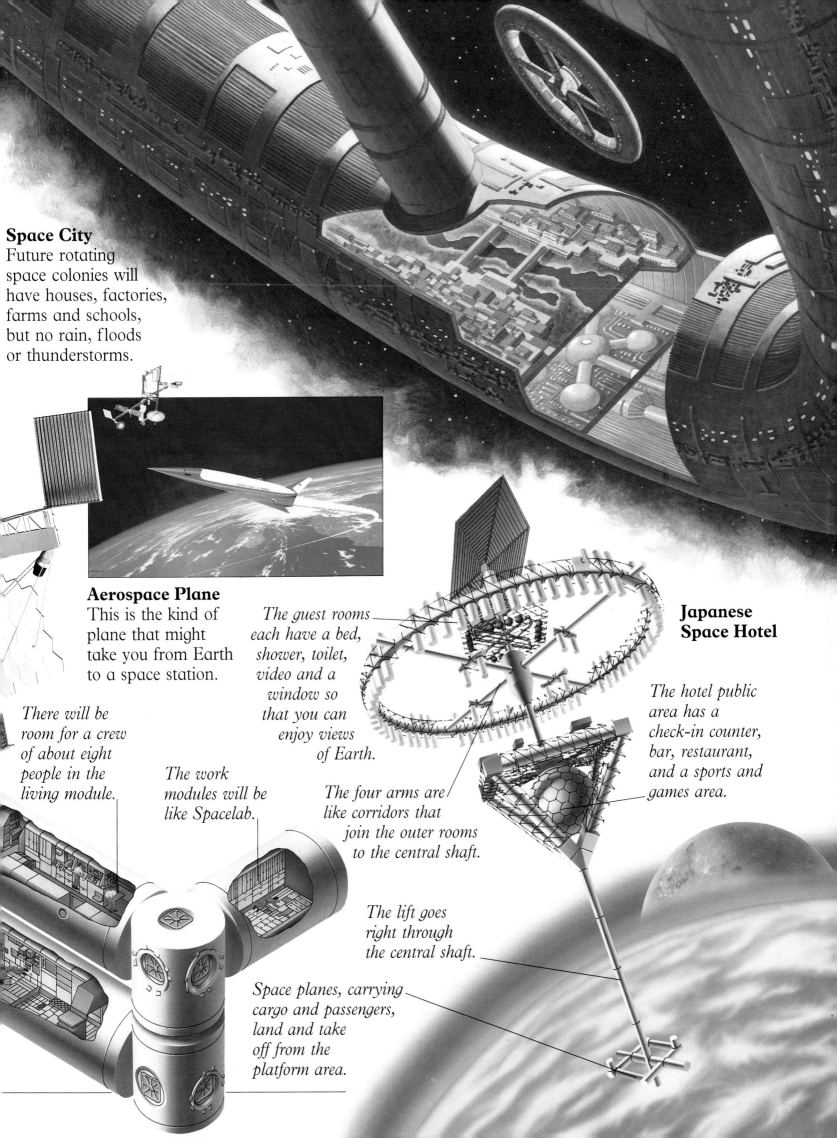

Space City
Future rotating
space colonies will
have houses, factories,
farms and schools,
but no rain, floods
or thunderstorms.

Aerospace Plane
This is the kind of
plane that might
take you from Earth
to a space station.

The guest rooms
each have a bed,
shower, toilet,
video and a
window so
that you can
enjoy views
of Earth.

**Japanese
Space Hotel**

The hotel public
area has a
check-in counter,
bar, restaurant,
and a sports and
games area.

There will be
room for a crew
of about eight
people in the
living module.

The work
modules will be
like Spacelab.

The four arms are
like corridors that
join the outer rooms
to the central shaft.

The lift goes
right through
the central shaft.

Space planes, carrying
cargo and passengers,
land and take
off from the
platform area.

LIVING IN SPACE

A home on another planet may be a dream today, but it is quite possible that one day people will be living on the Moon or on Mars. The first settlements will be quite simple, and will be built under the surface. People will have to stay inside the protective buildings or wear a spacesuit, because there is no air and the radiation and meteorites make it dangerous.

The first people to go will probably be scientists and astronomers. Scientists think there are useful metals to be found there, and astronomers will build huge telescopes so that they can study the universe.

A Base on Mars

Solar panels will be used to convert the Sun's energy into power.

Nothing can grow on Mars unless it is in a special greenhouse. Water and air will need to be controlled.

Moon and Mars Mines
Aluminium, iron and other useful metals will be mined. The materials that are mined will be used where they are or taken back to Earth.

The inflatable dome is a temporary workshop used for repairing a Moon buggy.

Small moonlanders can be used as computer rooms.

Solar panels convert the energy from the Sun into electricity. Any extra electricity that is collected will be stored and can be used at night.

The Mars landing craft will not be wasted, but will be turned on their sides and used as Martian houses and workplaces.

Moon City
A team go out from their large city to explore the surface of the Moon.

Dust Gliding
Unlike the Moon, Mars has dust storms which give the sky a red glow. Perhaps gliders will be used for travelling in the Martian winds.

THE FUTURE

No one knows if there is life in other galaxies, or even elsewhere in our own galaxy. Many people claim to have seen alien spacecraft, which are sometimes known as UFOs (Unidentified Flying Objects), or flying saucers. Some people say they have even met the aliens who came from them!

To find out if there really are any aliens, astronomers listen for radio messages from space, and even send out their own, hoping that one day they will get an answer!

Starship
Huge spacecraft may travel long distances from Earth, through the galaxies, searching for other life.

Robot Traveller
In the future, robot vehicles will be specially made to land and move around easily on the rocks and craters of other planets.

Call the Garage
If your spacecraft broke down on another planet it would be much too dangerous to leave the safety of your craft. Robots would be used to repair it.

Ramscoop

This is a ramscoop starship. It has been damaged on its journey and is returning to its planet for repairs. There is life on this planet – but is it human life?

The Visitor

Has this strange creature just arrived on Earth? Is the spacecraft in the sky full of friendly aliens?

Space Strangers

A planet with water might have some form of fishy-insect life.

Creatures on a planet with low gravity might keep on growing and have long, skinny arms and fingers.

On a planet with a stronger pull of gravity, the creatures might be squashed towards the ground.

Floating Homes

Life in this space city would be like life on Earth, except that this city can be moved to another planet.

GLOSSARY

Antenna An aerial for transmitting or receiving radio signals.

Asteroid A small rock or metal object that orbits the Sun like a tiny planet. Most are in a belt between Mars and Jupiter.

Astronaut A person who travels beyond the Earth and into space.

Astronomer A person who studies the stars, planets and other objects in space.

Atmosphere A blanket of gases which surrounds a planet or moon.

Barred spiral galaxy A group of stars collecting together to make a spiral shape with a bar across the centre.

Command module The cone-shaped capsule in which the astronauts travelled during the Moon missions.

Comet An object in the solar system, made of ice and dust, which shines as it gets near to the Sun.

Constellation The pattern made by a group of stars in the night sky.

Cosmonaut The Russian word for astronaut.

Eccentric orbit When a satellite passes low over one side of the Earth and high over the other.

Eclipse When the shadow of one planet or moon falls on another.

Elliptical galaxy A huge group of stars collecting together to make an egg-like shape.

Equator The imaginary line around a planet halfway between the North and South poles.

Galaxy A huge 'island' of stars in space.

Geostationary orbit When a satellite is directly over the Equator, travelling in the same direction and at the same speed as the Earth.

Gravity The force of a planet which tries to pull everything towards its centre.

Hemisphere Half of a sphere. The Earth is divided into the northern and southern hemispheres by the equator.

Light-year The distance travelled by a beam of light in one year.

Lunar To do with the Moon.

Lunar module The craft used by the Apollo astronauts to land on the Moon.

Manned Manoeuvring Unit A small jet-pack worn by astronauts so that they can move around easily out in space.

Meteor A chunk of rock or metal which burns up as it falls through the Earth's atmosphere. Sometimes called a shooting star.

Meteorite A meteor which does not burn up and which reaches the ground.

Moon The natural satellite of a planet.

Observatory A place where astronomers go to study the night sky.

Orbit The path taken by one object around another such as the Earth around the Sun.

Planet A large round object that orbits a star. The Earth is one of the nine planets around the Sun. Planets do not shine but they reflect the Sun's light.

Polar orbit When a satellite passes over the North and South poles.

Pulsar A rapidly spinning star that gives off pulses of radio waves.

Quasar A very bright, distant object which may be the centre of a far-away galaxy.

Rocket A very powerful engine to launch people and objects into space.

Satellite A small object that circles round a larger one – either natural or man-made.

Service module The part of the Saturn 5 rocket which carried the engine, fuel and supplies for the Apollo Moon missions.

Solar To do with the Sun.

Solar panel The outside part of a satellite which is covered in cells that change sunlight into electricity.

Solar system The family of the Sun including the planets, moons, asteroids, meteors and comets.

Space probe A craft with no people in it that travels into space to explore the planets.

Space Shuttle A space plane that carries astronauts to work in space, and is re-usable.

Space Station A large structure in space where astronauts live and work for long periods of time.

Spacelab A workshop carried into space by the Space Shuttle.

Spacesuit A special suit worn by astronauts when they go spacewalking. It protects them from the dangers in space and supplies them with oxygen to breathe.

Spiral galaxy A huge group of stars together making a spiral shape.

Star A huge ball of burning gas giving out heat and light. Our Sun is a medium-sized star.

Supernova A huge star that explodes and blows itself apart.

Telescope A tube, with mirrors and lenses, to look through, which makes far-away objects look closer and bigger.

UFO Unidentified Flying Object A mysterious object in the sky that no one can explain.

Universe Everything that exists in space.

Weightlessness In space there is no gravity so things seem to have no weight and float around.

INDEX

Acknowledgments
Photography: Tina Chambers; Geoff Dann; Steve Gorton; James Stevenson.

Illustrations: David Bergen; Bob Corley; Tony Gibbons; Mick Gillah; Terry Hadler; Keith Hume; Chris Lyon; Sebastian Quigley; Roger Stewart; Grose Thurston; Graham Turner.

Models: Atlas Models; Peter Griffiths.

Thanks to: ESA; London Planetarium; The Science Museum, London; Truly Scrumptious Child Model Agency.

Picture credits
Genesis Space Photo Library: 16; **Michael Holford:** 36c; **Image Bank:** Dave Archer endpapers; **NASA:** front cover c, clb & crb, 3l, 5tr(3), 11l, 13t & b, 15, 17b, 20/21, 23, 24t, c, bl & br, 27b, 28b, 29t, 31t & b, 32t, 33t & b, 35b, 37b, 38c, 39cr, 43cl; **Science Photo Library:** 5tr(2), 26t, 39tr, Julian Baum 45c & b, Dr. Martin N. England 5b(2), 41br, Dr. Fred Espenak front cover cra, 4br, 26b, 41cr, David A. Hardy 41c, 46b, 47t & b, Kapteyn Laboratorium 38b, Dr.John Lorre 5b(1), 41ucr, NASA 3br, 27t, 35t, 36b, 44c, NASA/Dr. Gene Feldman/GSFC 20t, NOAO 40b, Mark Paternostro 47r, Max Planck Institute 38t, Ronald Royer 40/41, John Sanford 5tr(1), 8, 9, 37 t & r, 39tl, Dr. Rudolph Schild/Smithsonian Astrophysical Observatory 40t, US Naval Observatory 39br; **Tass:** 17t; **Telegraph Colour Library:** Space Frontiers 11r, 21b, Space Frontiers/N.R.S.C. 21t.

t – **top**   l – **left**   a – **above**   cb – **centre below**
b – **bottom**   r – **right**   u – **under**   c – **centre**   clb – **centre left below**
crb – **centre right below**   cra – **centre right above**

The
HELEN OXENBURY
Nursery Treasury

Illustrated by Helen Oxenbury
with rhymes compiled by Brian Alderson

BCA
LONDON · NEW YORK · SYDNEY · TORONTO

This edition published 1991 by
BCA
by arrangement with William Heinemann Ltd.

This collection published 1992
The Helen Oxenbury Nursery Story Book first published 1985
The Helen Oxenbury Nursery Rhyme Book first published 1986
Illustrations by Helen Oxenbury © 1974, 1985, 1986
Rhymes compiled by Brian Alderson © 1974, 1986

CN 4926

Printed in Belgium by
Proost International Bookproduction

Contents

The Three Little Pigs

Once there were three little pigs who grew up and left their mother to find homes for themselves.

The first little pig set out, and before long he met a man with a bundle of straw.

"Please, Man," said the pig, "will you let me have that bundle of straw to build my house?"

"Yes, here, take it," said the kind man.

The little pig was very pleased and at once built himself a house of straw.

He had hardly moved in when a wolf came walking by, and, seeing the new house, knocked on the door.

"Little pig, little pig," he said, "open up the door and let me in."

Now the little pig's mother had warned him about strangers, so he said, "No, not by the hair of my chinny-chin-chin, I'll not let you in."

"Then I'll huff and I'll puff and I'll blow your house down!" cried the wolf.

But the little pig went on saying, "No, not by the hair of my chinny-chin-chin, I'll not let you in."

So the old wolf huffed and he puffed and he blew the house down, and ate up the little pig.

The second little pig said good-bye to his mother and set out. Before long he met a man with a bundle of sticks.

"Please, Man," he said, "will you let me have that bundle of sticks to build my house?"

"Yes, you can have it. Here it is," said the kind man.

So the second little pig was very pleased and used the sticks to build himself a house. He had hardly moved in when the wolf came walking by and knocked at the door.

"Little pig, little pig," he said, "open up your door and let me in."

Now the second little pig remembered what his mother had told him, so he, too, said, "No, not by the hair of my chinny-chin-chin, I'll not let you in."

"Then I'll huff and I'll puff and I'll blow your house down!" cried the wolf.

But the little pig went on saying, "No, not by the hair of my chinny-chin-chin, I'll not let you in!"

So again, the old wolf huffed and he puffed, and he

huffed and he puffed. This time it was much harder work but, finally, down came the house and he ate up the second little pig.

Then, last of all, the third little pig set out and met a man with a load of bricks.

"Please, Man," he said, "will you let me have that load of bricks to build my house?"

"Yes, here they are – all for you," said the kind man.

The third little pig was very pleased, and built himself a brick house.

Again the wolf came along, and again he said, "Little pig, little pig, open your door and let me in."

But, like his brothers, the third little pig said, "No, not by the hair of my chinny-chin-chin, I'll not let you in."

"Then I'll huff and I'll puff and I'll blow your house down!" cried the wolf.

And when the third little pig wouldn't open the door, he huffed and he puffed, and he huffed and he puffed. Then he tried again but the brick house was so strong that he could not blow it down.

This made the wolf so angry that he jumped onto the roof of the little brick house and roared down the chimney, "I'm coming down to eat you up!"

The little pig had put a pot full of boiling water on the fire and now he took off the lid. Down the chimney tumbled the wolf and – SPLASH – he fell right into the pot.

Quickly, the little pig banged on the cover and boiled up the old wolf for his dinner.

And so the clever little pig lived happily ever after.

Henny-Penny

One day when Henny-Penny was scratching about for corn in the farmyard, an acorn fell down from the oak tree and hit her on the head.

"Goodness gracious," she cried, "the sky is falling. I must go and tell the king."

So, off she went in a great hurry and soon she met Cocky-Locky.

"Where are you going?" asked Cocky-Locky.

"I'm going to tell the king the sky is falling," said Henny-Penny.

"Can I come, too?" asked Cocky-Locky.

"Yes, do," said Henny-Penny.

So off went Henny-Penny and Cocky-Locky to tell the king the sky was falling, and, before long, they met Ducky-Daddles.

"Where are you going?" asked Ducky-Daddles.

"Oh, we're going to tell the king the sky is falling," said Henny-Penny and Cocky-Locky.

"Can I come, too?" asked Ducky-Daddles.

"Yes, do," said Henny-Penny and Cocky-Locky.

So off went Henny-Penny, Cocky-Locky and Ducky-Daddles to tell the king the sky was falling and, before long, they met Goosey-Poosey.

"Where are you going?" asked Goosey-Poosey.

"Oh, we're going to tell the king the sky is falling," said Henny-Penny, Cocky-Locky and Ducky-Daddles.

"Can I come, too?" asked Goosey-Poosey.

"Yes, do," said Henny-Penny, Cocky-Locky and Ducky-Daddles.

So off went Henny-Penny, Cocky-Locky, Ducky-Daddles and Goosey-Poosey to tell the king the sky was falling and, before long, they met Turkey-Lurkey.

"Where are you going?" asked Turkey-Lurkey.

"Oh, we're going to tell the king the sky is falling," said Henny-Penny, Cocky-Locky, Ducky-Daddles and Goosey-Poosey.

"Can I come, too?" asked Turkey-Lurkey.

"Yes, do," said Henny-Penny, Cocky-Locky, Ducky-Daddles and Goosey-Poosey.

So off went Henny-Penny, Cocky-Locky, Ducky-Daddles, Goosey-Poosey and Turkey-Lurkey to tell the king the sky was falling.

They went along together, Henny-Penny, Cocky-Locky, Ducky-Daddles, Goosey-Poosey and Turkey-Lurkey – along and along, until they met Foxy-Woxy.

"Where are you going?" asked Foxy-Woxy.

"Oh, we're going to tell the king the sky is falling," said Henny-Penny, Cocky-Locky, Ducky-Daddles, Goosey-Poosey and Turkey-Lurkey.

"But you're not going the right way," said Foxy-Woxy. "I know the right way. Let me show you."

"Thank you," said Henny-Penny, Cocky-Locky, Ducky-Daddles, Goosey-Poosey and Turkey-Lurkey.

So off they all went with Foxy-Woxy leading the way, and, before long, they came to a dark hole. Now this was really the home of Foxy-Woxy but he said, "This is the shortest way to the king's palace. Follow me."

So Foxy-Woxy went a little way down the hole and waited for Henny-Penny, Cocky-Locky, Ducky-Daddles, Goosey-Poosey and Turkey-Lurkey.

First came Turkey-Lurkey.

"Snap!" Foxy-Woxy bit off Turkey-Lurkey's head.

Next came Goosey-Poosey.

"Snap!" Foxy-Woxy bit off Goosey-Poosey's head.

Next came Ducky-Daddles.

"Snap!" Foxy-Woxy bit off Ducky-Daddles's head.

Next came Cocky-Locky.

"Snap!" But this time Foxy-Woxy was getting tired and he missed, so that Cocky-Locky managed to call out to Henny-Penny, "Look out! Don't come!"

Henny-Penny heard Cocky-Locky and ran back home to the farmyard as fast as she could go. And that was why she never told the king the sky was falling.

———————◆———————

Hey! diddle, diddle,
The cat and the fiddle,
The cow jumped over the moon;
The little dog laughed
To see the sport,
While the dish ran after the spoon.

23

Baa, baa, black sheep,
    Have you any wool?
Yes, marry, have I,
    Three bags full:

One for my master,
    And one for my dame,
But none for the little boy
    Who cries in the lane.

24

The Little Red Hen

Once there was a pretty, neat little house. Inside it lived a Cock, a Mouse and a Little Red Hen.

On another hill, not far away, was a very different little house. It had a door that wouldn't shut, windows that were dirty and broken, and the paint was peeling off. In this house lived a bad old mother Fox and her fierce young son.

One morning the mother Fox said, "On the hill over there you can see the house where the Cock, the Mouse and the Little Red Hen live. You and I haven't had very much to eat for a long time, and everyone in that house is very well fed and plump. They would make us a delicious dinner!"

The fierce young Fox was very hungry, so he got up at once and said, "I'll just find a sack. If you will get the big pot boiling, I'll go to that house on the hill and we'll have that Cock, that Mouse and that Little Red Hen for our dinner!"

Now on the very same morning the Little Red Hen got up early, as she always did, and went downstairs to get the breakfast. The Cock and the Mouse, who were lazy, did not come downstairs for some time.

"Who will get some sticks to light the fire?" asked the Little Red Hen.

"I won't," said the Cock.

"I won't," said the Mouse.

"Then I'll have to do it myself," said the Little Red Hen. So off she ran to get the sticks.

When she had the fire burning, she said, "Who will go

and get the kettle filled with water from the spring?"

"I won't," said the Cock again.

"I won't," said the Mouse again.

"Then I'll have to do it myself," said the Little Red Hen, and off she ran to fill the kettle.

While they were waiting for their breakfast, the Cock and the Mouse curled up in comfortable armchairs. Soon they were asleep again.

It was just at this time that the fierce young Fox came up the hill with his sack and peeped in at the window. He stepped back and knocked loudly at the door.

"Who can that be?" said the Mouse, half opening his eyes.

"Go and find out, if you want to know," said the Cock crossly.

"Perhaps it's the postman," said the Mouse to himself. So, without waiting to ask who it was, he lifted the latch and opened the door.

In rushed the big fierce Fox!

"Cock-a-doodle-do!" screamed the Cock as he jumped onto the back of the armchair.

"Oh! Oh! Oh!" squeaked the Mouse as he tried to run up the chimney.

But the Fox only laughed. He grabbed the Mouse by the tail and popped him into the sack. Then he caught the Cock and pushed him in the sack too.

Just at that moment, in came the Little Red Hen, carrying the heavy kettle of water from the spring. Before she knew what was happening, the Fox quickly snatched her up and put her into the sack with the others. Then he tied a string tightly around the opening. And, with the sack over his shoulder, he set off down the hill.

The Cock, the Mouse and the Little Red Hen were bumped together uncomfortably inside the sack.

The Cock said, "Oh, I wish I hadn't been so cross!"

And the Mouse said, "Oh, I wish I hadn't been so lazy!"

But the Little Red Hen said, ''It's never too late to try again.''

As the Fox trudged along with his heavy load, the sun grew very hot. Soon, he put the sack on the ground and sat down to rest. Before long he was fast asleep. Then, ''Gr––umph . . . gr––mph,'' he began to snore. The noise was so loud that the Little Red Hen could hear him through the sack.

At once she took her scissors out of her apron pocket and cut a neat hole in the sack. Then out jumped: first the Mouse, then the Cock, and last, the Little Red Hen.

''Quick! Quick!'' she whispered. ''Who will come and help me get some stones?''

"I will," said the Cock.

"And I will," said the Mouse.

"Good," said the Little Red Hen.

Off they went together and each one brought back as big a rock as he could carry and put it into the sack. Then the Little Red Hen, who had a needle and thread in her pocket too, sewed up the hole very neatly.

When she had finished, the Little Red Hen, the Cock and the Mouse ran off home as fast as they could go. Once inside, they bolted the door and then helped each other to get the best breakfast they had ever had!

After some time, the Fox woke up. He lifted the sack onto his back and went slowly up the hill to his house.

He called out, "Mother! Guess what I've got in my sack!"

"Is it – can it be – the Little Red Hen?"

"It is – and the Cock – and the Mouse as well. They're very plump and heavy so they'll make us a splendid dinner."

His mother had the water all ready, boiling furiously in a pot over the fire. The Fox undid the string and emptied the sack straight into the pot.

Splash! Splash! Splash! In went the three heavy rocks and out came the boiling hot water, all over the fierce young Fox and his bad old mother. Oh, how sore and burned and angry they were!

Never again did those wicked foxes trouble the Cock, the Mouse and the Little Red Hen, who always kept their door locked, and lived happily ever after.

One, two,
Buckle my shoe;

Three, four,
Shut the door;

Five, six,
Pick up sticks;

Seven, eight,
Lay them straight;

Nine, ten,
A good fat hen;

Eleven, twelve,
Who will delve;

Thirteen, fourteen,
Maids a-courting;

Fifteen, sixteen,
Maids a-kissing;

Seventeen, eighteen,
Maids a-waiting;

Nineteen, twenty,
My stomach's empty.

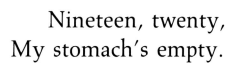

When good king Arthur ruled this land,
    He was a goodly king;
He stole three pecks of barley-meal,
    To make a bag-pudding.

A bag-pudding the king did make,
    And stuff'd it well with plums;
And in it put great lumps of fat,
    As big as my two thumbs.

The king and queen did eat thereof,
    And noblemen beside;
And what they could not eat that night,
    The queen next morning fried.

When Jacky's a very good boy,
    He shall have cakes and custard;
When he does nothing but cry,
    He shall have nothing but mustard.

The Turnip

Once there was a man who lived with his wife and little boy in a cottage in the country. One morning in May the man planted some turnip seeds.

Before long little turnip leaves began to poke up through the brown earth. Then an odd thing happened. One turnip plant began to grow faster than all the rest. It grew and it grew and it grew.

"We must have that turnip for supper tonight," said the man.

So he tried to pull the big turnip out of the ground. He pulled and he pulled and he pulled. But the turnip stuck fast.

"Wife, wife," he called, "come and help me pull this great turnip."

His wife came running. Then she pulled the man, and the man pulled the turnip. Oh how hard they pulled! But the turnip stuck fast.

"Son, son," called his mother, "come and help us pull this big turnip out of the ground."

The little boy came running and took tight hold of his mother. Then the boy pulled his mother, his mother pulled his father, and his father pulled the turnip. But still it stuck fast.

Then the little boy whistled for his dog.

"Come and help us," the boy said.

So the dog pulled the boy, the boy pulled his mother, his mother pulled his father and his father pulled the turnip. But still it stuck fast.

Then the dog barked for the hen.

The hen came flying and grabbed tight hold of the dog's tail. Then she pulled the dog, the dog pulled the boy, the boy pulled his mother, his mother pulled his father, and his father pulled the turnip. But still the turnip stuck fast.

"Cluck, cluck, cluck!" cried the hen.

And the cock came flying to help. Then the cock pulled the hen, the hen pulled the dog, the dog pulled the boy, the boy pulled his mother, his mother pulled his father, his father pulled the turnip and . . .

Whoosh! . . . Up came the turnip out of the ground, and down, backwards, they all tumbled in a heap. But they weren't hurt a bit and just got up laughing.

Then they rolled the turnip into the house and the boy's mother cooked it for their supper. Everyone had all they could eat and still there was enough left over for the next day, and the next, and the day after that!

The Elves and the Shoemaker

Once there was a shoemaker who lived with his wife in a little cottage. They were poor and he found it hard to earn enough money to live on.

Finally the day came when they had no money and only a crust of bread for supper. However, there was just enough leather left to make one pair of shoes. The shoemaker cut out the pieces carefully and put them on his workbench ready to sew together in the morning.

He woke early next day and went to his bench to make his last pair of shoes. But instead of the pieces of leather he had left the night before, he found a finished pair of shoes. They were more beautiful than any the shoemaker had ever made.

"Wife, wife!" he called excitedly. "Come and tell me if I'm dreaming!"

At this his wife came running and when she looked, she cried, "Oh, no, you aren't dreaming. The shoes are finished and . . . and . . . oh, so beautiful, too!"

While the shoemaker and his wife were turning the shoes around in their hands to see the fine stitches, a grand gentleman came in. He saw the lovely new shoes and wanted to buy them then and there. What is more, he paid the shoemaker so much for them that the shoemaker was able to buy leather for two more pairs. He also bought some fresh bread, cheese and other good food.

In the afternoon he cut out the new leather carefully and put the pieces on his workbench ready to sew together in the morning. Then he and his wife sat down

together for the best meal they had had for a long time. They went to bed very happy and slept soundly.

When they woke up next day, lo and behold, there were two new pairs of shoes, all sewn and shining on the

workbench. That same day the grand gentleman came to buy shoes for all his family and took both of the new pairs. The shoemaker was able to buy enough leather for four more pairs, and there was money left over, too.

Again on the third night the same thing happened and in the morning they woke up to find four new pairs of lovely shoes. Then more friends of the grand gentleman came and every pair was gone in a twinkling. This went on from day to day until the shoemaker and his wife were growing rich.

One morning the shoemaker's wife said, "We must try to find out who is being so kind so we can thank him."

"I know what we'll do," said the shoemaker. "Tonight we'll stay up and watch to see what happens."

So that night they hid themselves in a corner of the room and waited.

At midnight they heard the front door open and then they saw two little naked elves come dancing in. The elves sat down at once and began to sew so fast that, in only a few moments, there was a whole row of perfect new shoes and every single piece of leather had been used. Then the elves climbed down from the bench and ran out the door.

Next morning the shoemaker's wife said, "Now that we know who is helping us perhaps we can thank them in some way. I think they look cold without any clothes, poor things. I'm going to make them each a jacket and trousers and knit them some warm socks. It is getting colder every day and when the winter comes they will be frozen."

"What a good idea," said her husband, "and I will make them each a special pair of shoes."

They both set to work that very day but it took them some time because they had to stay awake many nights and watch to make sure of the right size. At last it was Christmas Eve and the clothes and the shoes were finished. The shoemaker and his wife laid them out carefully on the bench instead of the usual pieces of leather. Then they stayed awake and listened for their little friends to come.

When the clock struck twelve slow strokes, the elves came dancing in. At first when they climbed on the bench they couldn't understand what had happened. Then one of them held up a little jacket and they both cried out, "Oh, look! Look! These are clothes to wear and they will just fit us!"

It took only a moment to put everything on, and last of all, they found two little pointed caps. Everything fitted so perfectly that the two little elves danced and sang with delight.

Then out of the door they ran, and after that Christmas Eve, they never came again. But all now went well for the shoemaker and his wife. They were never poor again but lived happily ever after.

Sing a song of sixpence,
  A pocket full of rye;
Four and twenty blackbirds
  Baked in a pie;

When the pie was opened
  The birds began to sing;
Wasn't that a dainty dish
  To set before the king?

The king was in his counting house
  Counting out his money;
The queen was in the parlour
  Eating bread and honey;

The maid was in the garden
  Hanging out the clothes,
There came a little blackbird,
  And snapped off her nose.

Jenny was so mad,
  She didn't know what to do;
She put her finger in her ear,
  And cracked it right in two.

Hector Protector was dressed all in green;
Hector Protector was sent to the Queen.
The Queen did not like him,
Nor more did the King:
So Hector Protector was sent back again.

There was a piper, he'd a cow;
  And he'd no hay to give her;
He took his pipes and played a tune,
  Consider, old cow, consider!

The cow considered very well,
  For she gave the piper a penny,
That he might play the tune again,
  Of corn rigs are bonnie!

The Gingerbread Boy

There was once a woman who hadn't any children of her own and wanted one very much. One day she said to her husband, "I shall bake myself a nice gingerbread boy. That's what I shall do."

Her husband laughed at this idea but that very morning she mixed the dough and rolled it. Then she cut out a little boy shape with a smiling mouth and two currants for eyes. When she had popped him in the oven, she waited for him to bake and then she opened the door. Out jumped the gingerbread boy and ran away through the kitchen and right outside.

"Husband, husband," called the woman as she ran after the gingerbread boy.

The man dropped his spade when he heard his wife call and came running from the field.

But when the gingerbread boy saw the woman and the man chasing him, he only laughed, running faster and faster and shouting:

> *"Run, run, as fast as you can,*
> *You can't catch me,*
> *I'm the gingerbread man!"*

On he ran until he met a cow.

"Moo! Moo!" called the cow. "Stop! Stop! I want to eat you."

But the gingerbread boy only laughed and ran faster than ever, shouting, "I've run away from a woman and a man and now I'll run away from you!

"Run, run, as fast as you can,
You can't catch me,
I'm the gingerbread man!"

The cow chased after him but she was too fat and couldn't catch him. He raced on until he came to a horse.

"Neigh! Neigh!" snorted the horse. "You look good to eat. Stop and let me gobble you up."

But the gingerbread boy only laughed and shouted, "I've run away from a woman, a man, and a cow, and now I'll run away from you!

"Run, run, as fast as you can,
You can't catch me,
I'm the gingerbread man!"

The horse galloped after the gingerbread boy but couldn't catch him. He raced on faster and faster until he came to some farmers in a field.

"Ho! Ho!" they cried. "Stop! Stop! and let us have a bite."

But the gingerbread boy only laughed and shouted, "I've run away from a woman, a man, a cow, a horse, and now I'll run away from you!

"Run, run, as fast as you can,
You can't catch me,
I'm the gingerbread man!"

The men joined in the chase but no one could catch the
gingerbread boy. He raced far ahead until he came to a

river and had to stop. There he met a fox who wanted
very much to eat him then and there, but he was afraid
the clever gingerbread boy might escape.

So he said politely, "Do you want to cross the river?"

"Yes, please," said the gingerbread boy.

"Well, then, jump on my back and I'll swim across."

"Thank you," said the gingerbread boy; and he did just
that.

When they were about halfway across, the fox said,
"The water is deeper here. I think you'd better crawl up
onto my neck."

"Thank you," said the gingerbread boy; and he did just
that.

When they had gone three-quarters of the way across,

the fox said, ''You'd better climb up onto my head. You can't be very comfortable there.''

''Thank you,'' said the gingerbread boy; and he did just that.

''We're nearly there now,'' said the fox a moment later. ''I think you'll be safer if you get onto my nice long nose.''

''Thank you,'' said the gingerbread boy. But no sooner had he climbed onto the fox's nose than the fox threw back his head and SNAP! went his big mouth.

The gingerbread boy was half gone.

Then the fox did it again, SNAP!

The gingerbread boy was three-quarters gone.

The fox was having a very good time, and he did it again. SNAP!

The gingerbread boy was all gone.

And that was the end of the gingerbread boy who had been too clever for the woman, the man, the cow, the horse, and the farmers. But not clever enough for the fox.

——————◆——————

What are little boys made of, made of,
What are little boys made of?
Snaps and snails and puppy-dogs' tails;
And that's what little boys are made of, made of.

What are little girls made of, made of,
What are little girls made of?
Sugar and spice, and all that's nice;
And that's what little girls are made of, made of.

The Little Porridge Pot

There was once a little girl who lived in a village with her mother. They were very poor and things got worse and worse until one day they found that there was nothing left to eat.

"I'll go into the forest and see if I can find some berries," the little girl said. And off she went.

She had not gone far when she met a very old woman who smiled at her. "I know that you are a good little girl and that you and your mother are poor and hungry. Here is a little pot to take home. Whenever you say to it, 'Cook, little pot,' it will fill itself full of delicious steaming porridge. When you have had all you can eat, you must say, 'Enough, little pot,' and it will stop making porridge."

The little girl thanked the kind old woman and took the pot home to her mother. They were both so hungry that they could scarcely wait to say, "Cook, little pot."

At once the pot was full of porridge. Then, when they had eaten all they could, the little girl said, "Enough, little pot," and it was empty again.

From that day on, the little girl and her mother were never hungry anymore, and they lived very happily for a while.

But one day when the little girl was out her mother wanted some of that delicious porridge all for herself. Carefully, she got the pot down from the shelf and said the magic words, "Cook, little pot." In a moment the pot was full.

The little girl's mother ate as much as she wanted. Then, suddenly, she screamed.

"Oh dear! Oh dear! I can't remember how to make it stop!"

The porridge kept on coming and coming. It filled the little pot to the brim. It seeped over the top and down onto the table. Bubbling and steaming, it overflowed onto the floor. More and more kept coming. The porridge ran across the floor and out of the door and streamed down the street. It went into neighbours' gardens! And into

their houses! Finally, there was only one house in the whole village that wasn't filled with porridge!

"Oh! Oh! Oh!" all the villagers cried at once. "Whatever shall we do?"

At that very moment, the little girl came home, and seeing porridge everywhere, she cried, "Enough, little pot."

To everyone's relief, the porridge stopped coming. However, they all had to squeeze into the one house that had escaped and live there together until, at last, they could eat their way back to their own homes.

Girls and boys, come out to play,
The moon doth shine as bright as day;
Leave your supper, and leave your sleep,
And come with your playfellows into the street.
Come with a whoop, come with a call,
Come with a good will or not at all.
Up the ladder and down the wall,
A halfpenny roll will serve us all.
You find milk and I'll find flour,
And we'll have a pudding in half an hour.

Little girl, little girl, where have you been?
Gathering roses to give to the queen.
Little girl, little girl, what gave she you?
She gave me a diamond as big as my shoe.

Pussy-cat, pussy-cat, where have you been?
I've been up to London to look at the queen.
Pussy-cat, pussy-cat, what did you there?
I frightened a little mouse under the chair.

71

Little Red Riding Hood

There was once a little girl whose mother made her a new cloak with a hood. It was a lovely red colour and she liked to wear it so much that everyone called her Little Red Riding Hood.

One day her mother said to her, "I want you to take this basket of cakes to your grandmother who is ill."

Little Red Riding Hood liked to walk through the woods to her grandmother's cottage and she quickly put on her cloak. As she was leaving, her mother said, "Now remember, don't talk to any strangers on the way."

But Little Red Riding Hood loved talking to people, and as she was walking along the path, she met a wolf.

"Good morning, Little Girl, where are you off to in your beautiful red cloak?" said the wolf with a wicked smile.

Little Red Riding Hood put down her basket and said, "I'm taking some cakes to my grandmother who's not very well."

"Where does your grandmother live?" asked the wolf.

"In the cottage at the end of this path," said Little Red Riding Hood.

Now the wolf was really very hungry and he wanted to eat up Little Red Riding Hood then and there. But he heard a woodcutter not far away and he ran off.

He went straight to the grandmother's cottage where he found the old woman sitting up in bed. Before she knew what was happening, he ate her up in one gulp. Then he put on the grandmother's nightdress and her nightcap, and climbed into her bed. He snuggled well

down under the bedclothes and tried to hide himself.

Before long, Little Red Riding Hood came to the door with her basket of cakes and knocked.

"Come in," said the wolf, trying to make his voice sound soft.

At first, when she went in, Little Red Riding Hood thought that her grandmother must have a bad cold.

She went over to the bed. "What big eyes you have, Grandmama," she said, as the wolf peered at her from under the nightcap.

"All the better to see you with, my dear," said the wolf.

"What big ears you have, Grandmama."

"All the better to hear you with, my dear," answered the wolf.

Then Little Red Riding Hood saw a long nose and a wide-open mouth. She wanted to scream but she said, very bravely, "What a big mouth you have, Grand-mama."

At this the wolf opened his jaws wide. "All the better to eat you with!" he cried. And he jumped out of bed and ate up Little Red Riding Hood.

Just at that moment the woodcutter passed by the

cottage. Noticing that the door was open, he went inside. When he saw the wolf he quickly swung his axe and chopped off his head.

Little Red Riding Hood and then her grandmother stepped out, none the worse for their adventure.

Little Red Riding Hood thanked the woodcutter and ran home to tell her mother all that had happened. And after that day, she never, ever, spoke to strangers.

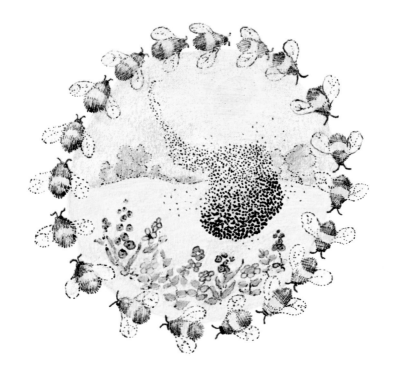

A swarm of bees in May
Is worth a load of hay;

A swarm of bees in June
Is worth a silver spoon;

A swarm of bees in July
Is not worth a fly.

Rosemary green,
And lavender blue,
Thyme and sweet marjoram,
Hyssop and rue.

Gray goose and gander,
　　Waft your wings together,
And carry the good king's daughter
　　Over the one strand river.

The Three Billy Goats Gruff

Once upon a time there were three Billy Goats. Their names were Big Billy Goat Gruff, Little Billy Goat Gruff and Baby Billy Goat Gruff.

They had lived all winter on a rocky hillside where no grass or flowers grew for them to eat. By the time spring came and the weather began to get warmer, they were thin and very hungry.

But over the bridge on the other side of the river the hillside wasn't rocky at all. There the grass was thick and green with delicious flowers growing in it.

"We must cross the bridge to the other side where we can find plenty to eat," said Big Billy Goat Gruff.

"But the wicked Troll who lives under the bridge won't let anyone cross," said Baby Billy Goat Gruff.

The Billy Goats Gruff were afraid to cross the bridge but it was the only way to reach the lovely grass. They grew hungrier and hungrier every day until one day they put their heads together and made a plan.

First Baby Billy Goat Gruff went down the hillside and started across the bridge.

"Who goes there?" cried the Troll.

"It's only me, Baby Billy Goat Gruff."

"I'll eat you up," screamed the Troll. "I eat anyone who dares to cross my bridge."

"But I'm so small I'm only a mouthful," said the littlest Billy Goat Gruff. "If you wait for my bigger brother, he'll be along in a few minutes."

"Oh, all right," said the Troll crossly.

So Baby Billy Goat Gruff went safely over the bridge.

Before long the next brother, Little Billy Goat Gruff, came to the bridge.

At once the Troll roared, "You can't cross my bridge. I'm going to eat you up!"

Little Billy Goat Gruff leaned over the side and called down to him, "I'm only a bit bigger than my baby brother and scarcely more than two mouthfuls. Wait for my big brother who will be coming along soon."

"Oh, very well then," said the Troll, "but I'm getting very hungry and I won't wait much longer."

Before the old Troll could change his mind, Little Billy Goat Gruff was across the bridge and away up the hill to join his brother.

It wasn't long before Big Billy Goat Gruff came down the hill and started to cross the bridge. At once the Troll jumped out from underneath and reached up to catch him. But Big Billy Goat Gruff was very strong and he butted the Troll hard with his great horns. He tossed him high in the air and then . . . splash ! . . . down . . . down he went, right into the middle of the river.

How Big Billy Goat laughed as he dashed across the bridge and up the hillside to join his two brothers.

Goldilocks and the Three Bears

Once upon a time, there were three bears who lived together in their own little house in the wood. There was a great big father bear, a middle-sized mother bear and a little baby bear. They each had a special bowl for porridge, a special chair for sitting in, and a special bed to sleep in.

One morning the mother bear made their porridge for breakfast and poured it out into the great big bowl, the middle-sized bowl and the little baby bowl. But it was so hot the bears decided to go for a walk while it cooled.

Now a little girl called Goldilocks was walking in the woods that morning and she came across the bears' house. She knocked on the door and when there was no reply, she crept slowly in.

"Oh! Oh!" she cried when she saw the bowls of porridge. "I'm so hungry; I must have just one spoonful."

First she went to the great big bowl and took a taste. "Too hot!" she said.

Then she went to the middle-sized bowl and tried that porridge. "Too cold," she said.

Last she went to the little baby bowl. "Oh! Oh! Just right!" she cried, and she ate it all up, every bit.

Then Goldilocks saw the great big chair and climbed into it. "Too big," she said, and climbed down quickly.

Next she went to the middle-sized chair and sat down. "Too hard," she said.

Then she went quickly to the little baby chair. "It just fits," she said happily. But really the chair was too small for her and – CRACK – it broke, and down she tumbled.

Then she went into the next room where she saw three neat beds. First she climbed into the great big bed, but it was too high. Next she climbed into the middle-sized bed, but it was too low.

Then she saw the little baby bed. "Oh! Oh!" she cried. "This is just right." She got in, pulled up the covers, and went fast asleep.

Before long the three bears came home for their breakfast. First the great big bear went to eat his porridge.

He took one look and said in his great rough voice, "Somebody has been eating my porridge!"

Then the middle-sized bear looked into her bowl and said in her middle-sized voice, "And somebody has been eating my porridge, too!"

Finally the little baby bear went to his bowl. "Oh! Oh!" he cried in his little baby voice. "Somebody's been eating my porridge and has eaten it all up!"

After that, all three bears wanted to sit down. The great big bear went to his great big chair and saw that the cushion had been squashed down. "Somebody has been sitting in my chair," he cried in his great big voice.

Then the middle-sized mother bear went to her middle-sized chair and found her cushion on the floor. "Somebody has been sitting in my chair," she said in her middle-sized voice.

Then the little baby bear hurried to his chair. "Oh! Oh!" he cried in his little baby voice "Somebody's been sitting in my chair and broken it all to bits!"

The three bears, feeling very sad, went into the bedroom.

First the great big bear looked at his bed. "Somebody has been lying in my bed," he said in his great big voice.

Then the middle-sized bear saw her bed all rumpled up and she cried in her middle-sized voice, "Oh dear, somebody has been lying in my bed."

By this time the little baby bear had gone to his little baby bed and he cried, "Somebody has been lying in my bed, and she's still here!"

This time his little baby voice was so high and squeaky that Goldilocks woke up with a start and sat up. There on one side of the bed were the three bears all looking down at her.

Now Goldilocks did not know that they were kind bears

and she was very frightened. She screamed, jumped out of bed, ran to the open window and quickly climbed out. Then she ran home to her mother as fast as she possibly could.

As for the bears, they put things to rights, and since Goldilocks never came again, they lived happily ever after.